LOSE YOUR QUIT

BY

DANNY CAHILL

Harrison House
Tulsa, OK

The Biggest Loser and NBC are not associated with this book or the information within in any way.

Scripture quotations are taken from the HOLY BIBLE, NEW INTERNATIONAL VERSION®. Copyright© 1973, 1978, 1984 Biblica. Used by permission of Zondervan. All rights reserved.

Lose Your Quit
ISBN: 978-1-60683-744-3
Copyright © 2012 by Danny Cahill
P. O. Box 2264
Broken Arrow, OK 74013-2264
www.TheDannyCahill.com
www.LoseYourQuit.com
danny@thedannycahill.com

Published by Harrison House Publishers
P.O. Box 35035
Tulsa, Oklahoma 74153
www.harrisonhouse.com

Also by Danny Cahill
Losing Big by Danny & Darci Cahill © 2012
Published by Harrison House Publishing, LLC

Dedication

This book is dedicated to my wife Darci and my children, David and Mary Claire, without whom I would have never been able to accomplish winning The Biggest Loser, and for whom I did so.

In memory of my incredible father, Charlie Cahill, or just "Dad" to me, who showed me that no matter the circumstances you find yourself in, you can choose differently and just not blame others for where you stand. If you don't like it, stand somewhere else.

To my mother, Sandra, who spent the last years of my father's life "losing her quit" by taking care of my father. Because of her love and dedication to him, he lived a long, incredible life.

To the fifteen incredible and life-changing souls who were on that ranch with me in Calabasas, California, inspiring me to change my life and to write new songs. Because of every one of you, I am soaring higher than I ever would have without you: Alexandra, Antoine, Sean, Julio, Dina, Coach Mo, Abby, Tracey, Daniel, Shay, Rebecca, Allen, Liz, Amanda, and Rudy.

And to God, for giving me the desire to change my life and the opportunity to change the lives of others through my motivational speaking and music. It was all for His cause that I've done any of it.

Contents

Foreword

When Danny and the Black Team went home in week six, I worried they'd struggle. The pressures at home are immense and the support is sometimes not there. The contestants are returning to find the same dysfunctional environment that enabled their unhealthy habits, and I actually expected that people could gain weight.

The weigh-in went somewhat as planned: Amanda lost six pounds, Shay lost five, Abby lost four and Dina lost five. When Daniel got on the scale, my fears were realized when it showed that he gained a pound. Then there was Danny C. When the scale showed 15 pounds lost - more than any other contestant on or off the ranch that week - I knew he had turned the corner and felt deeply confident that he would be successful with his weight loss and reclaiming his health. I took him aside and told him that he had "gotten" it.

Danny C began to realize that regrets hold you back, and that beating himself up over his past was pointless. He began to see his failures as entry points for learning and used these lessons to turn his life around.

Danny's journey on *The Biggest Loser* was a success, not only because he came into the house ready to change, but because his transparency and willingness to open up allowed him to make the discoveries needed to "right the ship" in his life. The fact that Danny holds the record for the highest percentage of body weight lost in the history of the show at 55.58%, for the most consecutive double-digit weight losses with seven weeks in a row, and was the first ever to lose more than 200 pounds before the show's finale should be proof that he has changed his life for the better.

On *Larry King Live* when Larry asked me if I was worried if Danny would gain the weight back, I confidently said, "Not this one." Danny had that epiphany he needed to not only change his weight, but to change his mind. Just as Suze Orman predicted that Danny would win the show, I can predict that any reader who opens *Lose Your Quit* will find much needed inspiration.

Lose Your Quit will take the reader through Danny C's life before and during *The Biggest Loser*, allowing them to apply his discoveries and realizations in their own life for the motivation to "Lose Their Quit."

Jillian Michaels

Introduction

It was hopeless. I remember it as if it were yesterday. I was sitting in my office in the back of the building working on one of the many overwhelming jobs on my list when I looked up at an old picture of me. I was 21 years old, I was 185 pounds and I was playing my bass guitar standing on a stage next to Donny Osmond. That night was amazing.

My sister Cathy had a crush on Donny Osmond at a very young age. I now see my daughter freaking out about Justin Bieber and I remember my older sister Cathy was the same about Donny! I also remember her record collection. There was a very old album of his called *The Donny Osmond Album*. My sister was a huge influence in my life, and just to be able to get this album signed for her was going to be an incredible gift. I was so excited to be able to do something for her that no one else could. After all, she had taught me to read, given

me my first penny, and pretty much raised me from birth! In fact, I think I was so much more proud of giving her that gift than playing music with Donny!

With the help of her roommate, I snuck into her house through a window and "borrowed" the album without her knowing. I took it to the Oklahoma City Fairgrounds where the KJ-103 Wild Weekend was being held and backstage I met Donny for the

first time. I told him of my plan and showed him the album. His reply was, "Wow! I haven't seen one of those in ages!" Cathy had carved, "I love you Donny" in the face of the album, as many young girls in the 70's did. When he signed the album, I felt so proud. We then went on stage and played to the thousands of people there and had a great time. Of course, my sisters were there in the crowd, and when I presented Cathy with the album after the gig, she was touched!

I say all of this because while most kids my age were playing in dive bars and parties, I was playing on stage in front of thousands of people. Music was natural to me; as natural as breathing was to live. In fact, at that time of my life, if you told me that at one point I would give it all up, I would have called you crazy!

> *Sometimes it was hard for others*
> *to tell I had lost hope; I always hid*
> *behind a smile. But unbeknownst to others,*
> *there was a war going on inside my head.*

But there I was; 38 years old, 460 Pounds, and feeling so hopeless. Sometimes it was hard for others to tell I had lost hope; I always hid behind a smile. But unbeknownst to others, there was a war going on inside my head. After I looked at that picture of me all those years ago playing music with Donny, my co-worker Glenn walked into my office. I

remember looking at him so frustrated. He asked me what was wrong and I said, "Why am I doing this? Why am I here in the back of this building in this office? This is not what I wanted to be doing 20 years ago! I wanted to be a musician! I have talent and I feel like I settled for making a living instead of making my dreams come true." His answer was simple as he answered with a question: "I don't know," he said. "You tell me?"

That knocked down a wall that had been built up for years; the wall that protected me from myself. You see, I blamed my situation on everyone and everything around me. I never stood up and took responsibility for my life. I felt like a victim instead of feeling I was in control of what happened to me. Right then and there I decided that I would no longer let others control my fate. If I was going to change my situation, I would have to own where I was and take action. Now if I told you that I knew that *The Biggest Loser* would be the avenue to my dreams coming true, it would be a lie. But if I told you that for the first time I felt a weight of ignorance lifted from my soul, it would be right on the money!

This was in early 2008, just before my life was transformed forever. I hadn't written a song in over 12 years. But years ago, that night I played for Donny Osmond, I remember taking the guitar player Drew back to my house after the show. I played what must have been a dozen tapes full of songs that I had written over the years; some okay, some pretty good, and some were just terrible; but I was living with passion and moving toward my dream. But in 2008, the only time I picked up my guitar was at my church to play praise and worship. That was the only way music was still a part of my life.

The next Sunday after I played the first church service, that short conversation I had with Glenn began to stir something inside me. I went into the music room and made my way back to the piano. I began playing some chords that were on my heart. I wrote some lyrics while waiting for the next service to begin and the rest is history. Those creative juices, and more importantly that belief in me, had returned. I wrote the song *King of Kings* and recorded it with my friend, John Conrad. It wouldn't be the last song I would write, but I didn't know that I would be 1500 miles from my family, sequestered from the world, and in the process of taking back that belief in me before I would find the inspiration to write my next one. And I would be completing a task that I never thought I'd have the chance to accomplish, and doing something that no other human on the planet had ever accomplished before.

Sometimes the smallest, most unexpected conversations can spark a fire that will forever burn bright and change the course of our future. I'm sure you've heard the saying, "hindsight is 20-20." This is because we seldom are able to see the big picture while we are on the journey. We see the small, single steps that take us from point to point; and those steps usually don't tell the whole story. In fact, they often seem insignificant. It can be like trying to read a story before it has ever been written! We end up confused and wondering if the path we took is the path we were destined to take.

I know that you have had times in your life when things felt hopeless; times when you asked yourself, "Why am I here?" Or perhaps you've asked, "Who am I?" Or even, "How will I ever get out of this mess?" Maybe you are in a relationship that seems hopeless or maybe you have been thinking of that dream that you let slip away.

I have good news for you. Although things may seem hopeless, they never are. Although that debt you have accrued seems like a mountain too high to climb, it isn't. Although the weight you have to lose may seem like too much to tackle, it's not. And although your marriage might seem like it might be beyond saving, it just might depend on you. And as my friend and former Pictures band mates once said in a song, "The secret to keeping your dreams alive is to hide them within your heart."

I promise you that dream is still there. It may be covered by some stuff that you need to sort through, but it's still there. Sure you've changed! If you hadn't, I'd say something was seriously wrong! But your desires and dreams can be awakened once again. You *can* be healthy and fit again; or for the first time in your life! You *can* start that business you've always dreamed of! You *can* save your marriage! You *can* reconcile with that loved one you haven't talked with in years! You *can* go back to school and get the degree you've always wanted! It *is* within your heart, and it *is* possible.

"The secret to keeping your dreams alive is to hide them within your heart." - **Pictures**

No, you are *not* too old, too fat, too weak, or too far gone. No, you are *not* too stupid, too lazy, or too tired. You just have to wake your heart up and get yourself back in the race! That dream is there, and it is up to you to make it happen. Once you decide you hold the keys to your future and the decision becomes "yes," it will be a *done deal*. But the fact remains that it will take *you* to make it happen. It will take *you* to do the work. It will take *you* to decide to change the physical course of your future. Yeah, it's scary. Yeah, it's the unknown. Yeah, it will require self-discipline. But I know something you may not. I know that *YOU CAN DO IT!*

After reading this book, I hope that you learn some of the things that I have learned; hopefully without having to go through the hell I had to go through to learn them! My goal and my purpose in writing this book is to wake that "something" up inside of you that you have either lost, forgotten about, or that you may be too afraid to even face. Believe me, I know what it's like to feel hopeless, to be scared, and to struggle on the way to success. But I do know that anything you want in life is possible.

Yeah, I know what you may be thinking. "It's easy for *you* to say, Danny. NBC isn't going to give me my own reality show to solve my problems!" Well, I can tell you that I have been through the fire more times than with just my weight. There is an untold story that you may not have heard about me; a story that includes addictions, debt, and hopelessness. There was a story that was never shown on NBC and *The Biggest Loser*. And I conquered each of those things using the same principles I used to win *The Biggest Loser*; and they are the same principles you can use in your own struggles. So I can tell you with complete honesty and confidence that you don't need a reality show to change your life. You just need to *change your mind.*

**You don't need a reality show to change your life.
You just need to change your mind.**

So go "palms up," as Bob Harper said that first day I was in the gym with him. Become teachable and willing to take a good hard look at your life. And above all else, be willing to change - because although you can't change everything in the world around you, you can change your world by changing you.

Most people want to change everyone else around them. A husband might say, "I wish my wife would change" while the wife says, "I wish my husband would change." An employee wishes their boss would change while the boss wishes the employee would change. But if you just figure out that the way to change your situations and your relationships is by first changing you, you will begin taking the first steps toward your dreams. So let's get started!

Had you told me a few years ago that I would be flying in an airplane around the world speaking to people about overcoming obstacles, I might have wondered if you were talking to the right guy! As I sat there in my office doing my day-to-day work as a land surveyor in Tulsa, Oklahoma, my mind would sometimes focus on all of my failures. The fact is, it had been years - even decades - since I had done anything that I thought of as heroic. Now, looking back at my life, I can see the treacherous road I traversed and all of the problems that I overcame. But being a 460-pound man caused me to see the biggest thing in the room: my failure with my health.

Let me paint you a picture. When I would sit down, there were several times I would *think* of getting up. I would run out of water, want to change the TV channel with the remote across the room, even have to go to the bathroom; but I would sit there and watch a program I didn't want to watch, hold my empty glass in thirst, and yes... even put off going to the bathroom! Why? Because until you've had 460 pounds of weight on your feet,  you just can't understand what it means just to get up out of your chair. It hurts; plain and simple. In fact, it was something I would avoid if at all possible! I would sit and wait until the reward would outweigh the pain before I would act. So there I was; sitting there *tolerating* a life that I was so unhappy with.

At work, I would wait to send all of my plots to the plotter. I knew as soon as I sent, them I would have to stand up, walk to the stairs, climb those stairs and retrieve my prints. Now to you this might not seem like such a big deal, but if you were as out of shape and obese as I was, it was *HUGE!* I was in a downward spiral and I had to stop. But the one

factor in the equation that would not cooperate was me. The less I moved, the more weight I gained. The more weight I gained, the more depressed I became. The more depressed I became, the more I ate and the more I ate, the angrier I became. I was angry at myself, but if you asked my family they would tell you I was angry at them. This is because those you are closest to are usually the

 ones you hurt the most. Few people knew this, because I would put on a face to the outside world; a face that smiled and seemed to be having a great time!

In fact, I once met my friend and pastor, Orlando Juarez, for lunch back in 2005. When I revealed to him I was thinking of getting Lap-Band surgery, his reaction was, "Why?"

When I recently asked him why he answered that way, he told me that he had never seen me as a 460-pound man. He said he always looked past my body and saw my spirit and how I went through life.

My ex-boss and friend, Dean Robinson, told me once recently, "Danny, you never were an unhappy man. You always seemed to be a pleasant person and full of life." My friend Tim once said, "You never carried yourself like an obese person. You acted as if it didn't bother you. On the golf course you never even walked like many obese people I've seen."

Introduction

The truth is that I put on my mask when I left the house and I began living a lie that would continue throughout the day. All of my frustrations would get stuffed into my heart and people would think nothing was wrong! Then I would pull into my driveway, "slide" out of my truck, lumber through the front door and explode on my family. They were confused as to why the world got nice, happy Danny while they got all of my rage. My wife and children continually walked on eggshells. They never knew when the eruption was coming, but there was always a plume of smoke billowing from my soul. It was only a matter of time.

I would often hide behind a façade of comedy. I once wrote a poem about my life and the last line was, "funny as I hide." There were times when completely embarrassing things would happen and I would make a joke about it! Once I was in a restaurant with co-workers and we all sat at the table. It was bad enough when the hostess would ask us, "Would you like a table or a booth?" I would often say, "Are your booths double extra wide?" I would hope this would bring giggles and hide the fact that everyone looked at me when they would ask the question. Well, needless to say we would always get a table.

That day as I sat in my chair, we all heard a strange, creaking noise. Just as we all looked around, two legs of my chair broke and it practically disintegrated beneath me! I crashed hard to the ground and the entire restaurant was silenced; that is except for the owner who came running across the restaurant screaming, "Are you okay?! Are you okay?!"

As my friends laughed, the owner was just worried that he might be getting sued! I can tell you that he had little to worry about; I'm sure that almost anyone could prove to a jury that those chairs weren't meant to hold 460 pounds! And I didn't even get angry at my friends for the laughter. I would have been a hypocrite. Too many times I have watched *America's Funniest Home Videos* and laughed like crazy as people fell on their faces over and over and over again!

Can you imagine what that did to my self-esteem? I was silently crushed over and over again. The more this happened the more I ate, and the more of my anger and wrath my family would receive. It was just a part of my life - a part that I didn't like but I chose to live with every day.

Now, just a few years later, I travel the entire world as a motivational speaker. Many times I speak about changing the very things that so many people are unhappy with in their lives. And before every speech or teaching, I play the same video. It is a two minute 43-second video that summarizes my journey on *The Biggest Loser*. It "tells the tale" of my journey on the show before I even walk out onto the stage.

I get emotional each and every time I am waiting for the video to end. Most of the time tears come; they come because I am about to do something I thought nearly impossible just a few years ago. I am about to stand up, walk up onto a stage in front of sometimes thousands of people, and stand up for an hour or more sharing my story. And the best thing is that I won't even think of sitting down.

In fact, I will remember that at one point in my life, I let it get so bad that I wouldn't even get out of my chair because it hurt.

People often ask me, "Danny, how could you have done that to yourself? How could you let it get so bad?" My answer: "Slowly. I slowly gave up on my dreams, I slowly gave up on my goals; slowly, I gave up on me."

People often ask me, "Danny, how could you have done that to yourself? How could you let it get so bad?" And my answer: "Slowly. Slowly I gave up on my dreams, slowly I gave up on my goals; slowly, I gave up on me." Just 17 years before that day, I sat in my office and went palms up. I was playing music and aspiring to have a career in music and the entertainment business.

My wife Darci will tell you that after our very first date, she returned home to tell her mother, "Get used to this one, Mom. He's the one I'm going to marry." Her mother was amazed! Darci was so fickle and even turned down dates from the most eligible bachelors! And here she was after a single date with a poor, starving musician, predicting her wedding day.

Now, that day came after numerous roadblocks and detours. In fact, we both almost called off the wedding numerous times. But the one thing Darci saw in me was a confidence that I had in myself. It was a confidence that I could do anything I set my mind to. Now, 17 years after we met, there I sat in my chair at my desk, procrastinating getting up and believing I could do *nothing*, much less *anything*.

Now I'll tell you that there's only one difference between me and many people out there, possibly even you, who have the same hopelessness I had. That one difference is that my lost dreams, unachieved goals, and the low self-esteem that resulted physically manifested into 460 pounds for the entire world to see. Others, and perhaps you, have the same kind of hurt, the same kind of unachieved goals and lost dreams, and the same low self-esteem that just hasn't physically manifested into something that we can all see. It's hidden deep down in your heart and soul and you, too, are putting on that mask before you walk out your door or into your church.

You are playing a role in a life that is not truly who you are and packing away all those feelings for the ones you love when you return home; or even worse, you are saving that rage for you. Maybe you hide an imaginary hammer under your bed so that when you get home and lay down you can reach underneath, grab the hammer, and commence to beating yourself up over and over again because of your failures.

Well, I have good news for you. Although it took me 17 years to get up to 460-pounds, it only took six months, three weeks and five days to take it *all* back off. So I promise you that if you decide to take ownership and responsibility for where you are in life and decide to change your mind, you can get back your dreams and goals a heck of a lot quicker than you lost them! In fact, for some of you, the journey to who you want to be will begin even before you finish reading this book!

Lose Your Quit

I've often heard people gripe and complain about their weight. They might say, "I've got to lose 40 pounds!" Are you kidding me? I had to lose 240 pounds! Now I know that 40 pounds, or even 10 pounds, is not easy to lose. I'm just trying to paint for you a picture of the task that was in front of me. It's like the difference between being $10,000 in credit card debt and $100,000 in credit card debt! While $10,000 is a huge task, $100,000 seems impossible. In fact, 240 pounds *did* seem impossible. Day after day, my thoughts had resigned that I would leave life early; it was just a matter of time. Would I see my children graduate high school? How would Darci take care of everyone after I died? As I popped my pile of pills that helped me with my high-blood pressure and edema, I would make sure my life insurance was paid up so that *when*, not *if*, I died they would at least be able to pay off the debt I had accrued! My life seemed hopeless.

One night at The Biggest Loser ranch, we received a call sheet. A call sheet tells us a little of what to expect the next day. It usually told us what to pack, how many meals to prepare, and gave us small hints of what was happening. This certain call sheet said to dress in sweats and a hoodie that we could move well in, and bring an extra pair of shoes. This usually meant there was a challenge. They said we'd be leaving just before dark and to be prepared for cool weather. What in the world were we going to be doing?! We would all look around at each other and make guesses about what was about to happen. The guesses were never even close!

We ended up at the beach just at sunset. It was beautiful, but it was getting cold and the ocean breeze was blowing. I remember wondering what we were going to do. Challenges and I just didn't mix. I hadn't done well in any of them! I was one of the biggest and perhaps the slowest person at the ranch! We lined up and began walking down the sandy beach. You have to imagine being close to 400 pounds and walking on the soft sand of Malibu Beach. You sink far down in the sand and walking is a task in itself.

When we finally walked around a corner, there stood Alison Sweeney. Now, one of three things was going to happen when we saw Ali: a weigh-in, a temptation, or a challenge. There were piles of sand with shovel handles sticking out of them. These were four-foot tall piles of sand! We were told our task was to get the shovel out of the sand and begin digging. There was a treasure chest buried beneath the sand and in it would be a key. Now, there isn't anything too complicated about that task, but that night was one of the most important nights of my life. It was the night I learned my first important lesson to achieving *anything* you want. And it was the night that my journey on *The Biggest Loser* changed forever.

You see, when you dig a hole in the sand - especially the soft sand of Malibu Beach - it doesn't just sit there in a pretty pile. And the hole you dig doesn't act like that old red clay I used to dig in

Oklahoma! When you get deep enough to see some progress, the sand from the side collapses and caves in on the work you've just done. So you dig some more, and it caves in again. You dig even some more, and it caves in again. I mean, after 15 minutes of digging as if my life depended on it, it looked like I had made no progress. This was going to take forever! And even then, I might not make it to the treasure chest.

While digging that night, I felt like quitting. I felt like giving up and resigning to the fact that the task was just too big. It felt like that mountain of weight I had carried around for years. Would I ever be free of the burden?

But that night something else happened. You see, there was something huge at stake. What Alison said made us realize the stakes. She said when we retrieved the key from the chest, it would open one of four locks. When all of the locks were opened, there was something inside that box. And she said only one thing about that something. She said, "What is inside that box is what will determine who will stay on the ranch, and who will be going home."

What? Could my existence on the ranch depend on this one moment in time! Could I be going home if I lost? Well, if there's anything you know about goals, it is that to reach your goal you need some sort of motivation. That motivation could be one of many things. It could be money, recognition, a cause, or even fear. The thought of leaving the ranch so early - just five weeks into my journey - terrified me. There was *NO WAY* I was going to let this send me home tonight! I had been put at risk, and I found my motivation behind the goal. I just kept digging.

Have you ever worked so hard on something only to see little, if any, results? Have you ever expended *so much* energy only to look and see you've only moved a fraction of an inch! Well, I have. I did for years trying to lose weight. Losing weight wasn't my problem! In fact, over the past 15 years I had lost 20, 30, or even 50 pounds several times! But let's face it; when you lose 50 pounds and *still weigh* 410 pounds, you just don't see much of a difference! So I would quit. I would give up and gain all of the weight back - and usually a few more pounds than I had lost!

But that night, with the fear of going home as my motivation, I never once stopped digging! Was it hard? Yup! Was it frustrating? Of course! In fact, seeing so little progress in my digging just ticked me off. But I had to keep on digging or my family was going to get 372–pound Danny back. Just the year before I went to *The Biggest Loser*, I lost weight down to 370 pounds! So, did I get on *The Biggest Loser* to do less that I had done before I went? *NO WAY!* I was going to make my family proud! I was going to show them what it takes to be a champion! I was going to lose this weight and live to see them grow up - live to grow old with my wife - live to see my grandchildren! So no matter what I *felt* like, I just kept digging and digging and digging until I reached my treasure chest and I pulled it out of the ground!

Now, at that point I heard something I hadn't heard before on The Biggest Loser ranch. I heard Alison Sweeney say, "Danny is the *first one* to get his treasure chest out of the ground!" In that one moment, I finally felt like I was making progress on my journey! I felt like there was a chance I might win this thing. There was a chance I could succeed and lose this weight! So I ran to the box and unlocked my lock. Now, there were three more to go. I had to get back and help my teammates dig up their chests so we would win this thing and stay on the ranch! But that wasn't going to happen. While I was skilled with a shovel - I worked on my uncle's paving crew as a mud cutter shoveling concrete and had dug up hundreds, if not thousands, of property corners over the years as a land surveyor - my teammates weren't quite as skilled. I scanned the three holes to figure out who I could help finish and increase our odds of winning only to see they were all only inches deep! So the Blue Team, our opponents, beat us in the first of our many losses to them in the challenges. I felt so defeated, humiliated, and frustrated.

When they opened the box, the Black Team and I waited to see what we had lost. They pulled out an envelope and we listened to the Blue Team scream with excitement! Then Alison Sweeney said, "You have won tickets home!" My heart sank, as I had been without my family for over 30 days! I wanted *so badly* to kiss my wife and hold my kids! But a thought then entered my head. *Why would I want to go home?* You see, Darci and I had made an agreement. My only job was to stay on that ranch as long as I could! I took the negative of losing a trip home to see my family for a week and turned it into a positive of realizing that in the long run, my family would be better off with me staying at the ranch!

That positive lasted about one minute when Alison Sweeney said, "But you have a choice, Blue Team. You can go home and see your families…or…you can stay here and keep your trainers on the ranch, The Biggest Loser gym, The Biggest Loser kitchen, and send the Black Team home to deal with the distractions." My heart sank as they chose to send *us* home.

I was ecstatic to see my family, but I was scared of leaving the ranch. I walked over to the hole I dug in the sand and looked into it. When I did, the sound of the waves seemed to disappear into the background. I barely heard anyone talking. It was like I was in a dream. I saw the walls of the sand and remembered just a few hours before how they kept caving in on all the work I was doing. I remembered feeling hopeless; like I would never be able to get to my treasure chest and get my key. Then I remembered what seemed like a thousand times when I lost 20 or 30…or even up to 50 pounds in the past! I would quit and give up because I would see so little results in the mirror. Then I would gain it all back! In fact, I added it up that night and, with a little mathematics, figured out I had lost almost a *half-ton* over the last 15 years! But I would always quit when I became discouraged. I always lost my motivation when I couldn't see results, because when you weigh 400+ pounds and you lose 20 pounds you just don't see any physical difference!

But what I didn't realize is that the physical manifestation of anything happens long after the mental decision not to quit! So all of those times I quit and gained all the weight back - all of the 15 years of work - was many times more work than it would have taken to lose the weight in the first place. I just needed to *LOSE MY QUIT!* I needed to decide to go the distance no matter what. I needed to learn that one step at a time added to the faith that your work is making a difference is the key. With that, you can reach your goal. The bigger the goal is, the longer the journey may be, but it has a destination that will be reached with tenacity, hard work, and *losing your quit!*

I just never made that decision. I lost my motivation and found my quit. Motivation is great, but it often won't last. You need to renew your motivation every single day of your life.

I didn't realize is that the physical manifestation of any goal happens long after the mental decision not to quit!

So many people run the 99-yard dash. They give up with one yard to go! If they saw the game from the press box they'd see the finish line, but when they're in the situation, they just don't see the details. That is where faith comes in. You only physically see the finish line moments before the end of a race. That is why you must visualize that finish line every moment of the race.

When Bob Harper worked me out on the ranch there was a sign. It said, "Believe in yourself. Trust the Process." You see, people always ask me, "Why can't I lose weight?" I dread giving them the answer. Not because I don't want them to know, but often they just don't want to hear the truth. The answer: If you eat healthy food in right portions and do the work, the weight will come off. The problem is usually both parts A and B of that equation. People want drive-thru food. People want monumental portions. There are restaurants that actually specialize in the "endless breadsticks" and "all you can eat buffets." And they stay in business for one reason: America loves it cheap, quick and easy. They don't want to mess with the details of weighing food and controlling what you eat. Many businesses don't want to follow the details. Accounting is an afterthought. Budget is a myth. And those companies will eventually fail because of the debt they will accrue.

Most people don't ever want to hear that it takes hard work. Leonardo Di Vinci once said, "O Lord, thou givest us everything at the price of an effort." Yes, anything worth having usually takes effort. And it usually takes hard work at that! I watch as people file

in and out of the gym, getting on the treadmill and turning it on only to grab it with both arms while they walk quite slowly. We had a guy on our paving crew once who would average about a shovel full every minute. Needless to say, his hole was always exponentially smaller than everyone else's. He promptly lost his job. You don't build great cities by doing a little work here and a bit of work there. Hoover Dam took six years to build during the Great Depression. Over 100 lives were lost during its construction. It wasn't a walk in the park; but it is a great wonder!

Have you ever seen the Grand Canyon from an airplane? It is an amazing sight. It is over 277 miles long, up to 18 miles wide, and over one mile deep. And it was all formed by a single river. The Colorado River and its tributaries are responsible for that great

wonder! Not a shovel of dirt was excavated by man to create it. But it took almost 18-million years to come to be. Slowly, the mighty Colorado River whittled away layer after layer of rock. The Colorado Plateau rose into the air because the river was busy with its work. What if that river had decided to stop? What if someone had turned off the water? Sounds funny, but that's what happens in businesses, relationships, and yes – even in weight loss. When the going gets tough and little results are seen, we usually quit. But that stubborn river carved out the greatest canyon on the face of the earth.

So I will tell you that if you want success in anything you do, the first requirement is that you become fully committed to finish. You just need to be *stubborn* like the Colorado River and decide quitting is not an option! You will most definitely find times when results aren't seen very quickly. But do you want results? Then commit yourself to the task no matter the circumstances. When one stops letting the circumstances of their life dictate their course of action, the work gets done. So you want results? Then you've got to *LOSE YOUR QUIT!*

Lose Your Regrets

Regrets are dangerous! They keep your concentration on the mistakes instead of the possibilities. I have read that a mistake only becomes a failure when you don't try again. Well, for 17 years straight, I wouldn't try again.

I never really gambled. Sure I played the occasional poker game with my friends. We played with nickels, dimes and quarters. No big deal. And every now and then we'd bet a few dollars on a game of 9-ball. But other than that, there wasn't much gambling at all.

It was 1993 and I opened the newspaper. On the sports page I saw the headlines: "Remington Park's 5th Anniversary." I remembered surveying some land around Remington Park, a horse racetrack, just before it was built in 1988. I casually stated to my father, "I've never even been to Remington Park." My father replied, "You've never been? You should go and experience it once. It is really a fun time!"

So Darci and I headed out to the track with her family for a day of fun. We got a table in the Silks restaurant and had a great time. As far as the gambling went, I won a few and lost a few. In fact, I think I left with only a few dollars lost. All in all, we had a great time! But a few weeks later on the way back from a college class, I passed by Remington Park. On a whim, I pulled off the highway. I entered the track and placed a few bets.

On the last race I put a $10 bet down on a trifecta bet. A trifecta bet is where you have to pick the 1st, 2nd and 3rd place winners in order, which is not an easy task! Well, I did and I won $780 that day! I hadn't seen that much money at once in a very long time! I

paid off some debt, picked up Darci from her work and we went out on the town! I felt great! I stopped in for just an hour or two and made a sweet $750!

Well, it didn't stop there. The casual trips to the track continued over the next year until I had given the $750 back to them, along with a few of my paychecks. But one day in November 1994, I handicapped the races and placed nine $4 Pick-Six tickets. A Pick-Six is almost like a lottery win! You have to pick the winner of 6 races in a row. The odds are astounding, but with all of the practice I had over the last year, I was able to lower the odds a bit. Well, one of my $4 tickets did well! In fact, it won $148,263.80 that day, along with several other wins. All in all, I walked in and bet just under $100 that day and walked out over $150,000 richer.

Now, a typical person would say that was the best day of their entire life! Not me. It was the worst day of my life. That was the day that gambling grabbed hold of me and wouldn't let go. I felt invincible! I felt like a champion! Boy did I have it down, and I bet that I could do it again! So I bought all kinds of gambling books. I bought books on blackjack, poker, craps, horse racing, roulette, and everything in between. I was going to beat the house. I spent plenty of time at Remington Park. I spent plenty of time playing poker. And I even flew back and forth to Las Vegas several times.

Now I can tell you by my own experience, they did not build Las Vegas on all of the winners. They built Vegas on all of us losers! So it wasn't too long before I turned a big win that should have bought me a house or a car into a mound of credit card debt for me and my family. The only thing was that my wife had no idea that I was gambling as much as I was. And I managed to keep it a secret for a long time!

In week five of *The Biggest Loser*, there was a temptation. And this time, it included a life-size roulette wheel. We had the option to play or we could sit it out. Now when I left for the ranch, Darci and I made an agreement. I was not to play any games at all. But when they announced the game, Darci wasn't there. She didn't hear what you could win! Here's how the game went.

If you opted in to play the game, you would step up to the wheel on your turn and give it a spin. It had to make at least one complete rotation and wherever the wheel stopped was your prize. Now, there could be one of several things hidden underneath the silver lids that were in each slot on the wheel: some money (which my family needed desperately), something you had to eat (which NONE of the Biggest Loser contestants wanted), or the *ULTIMATE* prize! Now, the ultimate prize was the "golden ticket." The golden ticket gave you the power to choose your teammates *and* your trainer! This was like stacking the deck and rigging a poker game! You were going to be able to give yourself four aces in your hand! It would make you virtually unbeatable!

Also, I knew which trainer I wanted – and which trainer I *DIDN'T* want! By the fifth week, you generally became attached to one trainer's method of workouts and also became emotionally close to that trainer. The last thing any of us wanted was to get the trainer we were least close to! And if you didn't get that golden ticket and the power to choose, you'd surely lose those friends you were closest to!

As an example, let's talk about putting a "Dream Team" together! Let's say it was in baseball. Say you were able to pick *any* player from *any* team and put them on *your* team! You could simply take the hottest and best players of the time and line them up in your dugout to dominate the competition! The best pitchers, hitters and the hottest manager in baseball! Think about it!

Well, on *The Biggest Loser*, you'd definitely want to pick the biggest guys who could lose the most weight. Rudy was humming along. His weight losses were amazing! He was shooting to be the first to 100 pounds lost in seven weeks, and he was over halfway there! You'd definitely pick Rudy! And there were others at the ranch that you'd definitely put on the team.

Well, there was no way I was going to let someone dictate whose team I was on! I still had that illusion of control we all have. We are never actually in control of what happens to us; we are only in control of how we respond. But at this point in my journey on *The Biggest Loser*, I wanted that control! So when Alison Sweeney asked who was going to play, I definitely took a step forward! And so did every other contestant – except one. Abby Rike stayed firmly where she was.

Abby Rike was a contestant on the show with me who had a tragic story. I remember sitting next to her in the finals week interview when she told her story. She explained how one evening she was having chest pains, and she had just had a baby. Her step daughter had a program that evening at school so her husband took the newborn and her daughter to the program. Abby told them she would go to the hospital to get checked out and meet up with them later. She was worried, but she tried not to let it show.

When she was about to leave the hospital after being checked out and given the green light, she tried to call her family. They wouldn't answer, which was not normal. She said her stomach knotted up and she felt like something was wrong. She drove home to see if everything was all right.

While driving home, she came upon a group of police cars and ambulances on the road. She immediately knew. She found out a short time later that an intoxicated driver going over 100 miles per hour hit the family vehicle head-on and killed her entire family. In an instant, her entire life was altered through no fault of hers. She told me later that she felt like she was supposed to be in that car with them, and the fact that she wasn't made her believe that she must have been spared death for something much bigger.

She decided not to play the game, because she knew that total control of your life was just an illusion. Although we claw and fight to control outside influences, we can never truly control everything that happens to us. We can only control how we respond to the events that happen. She said that the game wouldn't take her anywhere that she needed to go.

Well, I played, and so did everyone else except Abby! We all stepped forward and decided to take a spin on our future there. One reason most of us did was because Tracey Yukich decided to play. She had controlled almost every aspect of every game we had played thus far, and some of her decisions made some of the contestants really upset. My partner Liz and I didn't worry too much, as Tracy was our friend and we believed we had little to worry about.

We found out we were to spin according to our percentage of weight-loss thus far. Rudy stepped up and gave it a spin and immediately got the worst prize of them all: a thousand-calorie piece of cake! It was half his calorie intake for the entire day in one meal of refined sugar and fat! I felt relieved that I didn't get it! Next it was Rebecca's turn. She spun the wheel and it stopped on a Ding Dong. It was about 380 calories and, again, I was relieved! Then it was Allen's turn. As he spun the wheel, we all watched as he lifted the cover and it revealed a 100-calorie mini-cupcake. Abby was next, but she decided not to play, so now it was my turn to step up.

Being an analytical gambler, I did my calculations and decided I stood a great chance of winning! The prizes got significantly better each time, so surely the odds were in my favor to get a money prize, or perhaps even the golden ticket! Well, I spun the wheel and it was like the world was spinning in slow motion. All I could think about while the wheel spun was the agreement my wife and I made before I left for the ranch: *NO GAMES!* Just hard work and stay away from the game-play! Boy was I going to be in trouble when this aired on NBC!

The wheel slowed, and then stopped. I lifted the cover to reveal a cupcake. And not the 100-calorie cupcake that Allen ate; it was a 780-calorie cupcake that I had to eat! I was devastated! How could I have done this to myself? Why did I make the stupid decision to play that stupid game? Why didn't I just sit out! I should have known better. I gambled our family into great debt with my addictive behavior, and now I had gambled my way to possibly falling below the yellow line. What was I thinking?

Well, I forced that cupcake down and I walked back to my place in line. I was about to cry and punch myself at the same time! That feeling of weightlessness that I get when I make a mistake came to me and Abby noticed this. Then she asked me a question: "What's wrong, Danny?"

I replied: "I am *so stupid!* Why did I play? I always make the wrong decision and get myself into a hole! If I had just *not* played, I would be 780 calories ahead right now! I am so stupid!"

Abby then said something that would rock my world. She asked, "Would it have been the wrong decision had you got the golden ticket?" Immediately I thought to myself and answered, "Of course not! If I'd gotten the golden ticket it would have been a great decision!" As I said this, I looked over at Coach Mo who was looking at me out of the corner of his eye. He had the look of a concerned father when his son has made an error in judgment. The game then went on.

Tracey won the golden ticket the very next turn. We were all amazed! She spun the wheel once and it didn't complete an entire revolution. She had to spin it again and it landed on one of the four spaces that had already been hit. Her third spin was a charm and she won the golden ticket. Tracey, who was injured and desperate to control the game, gained the ultimate control. As everyone gasped and freaked out, I tried to look worried as Liz and I eyed each other and knew we'd be taken care of. Tracey was our friend!

Well, I was still beating myself up about making the wrong decision to spin that wheel as we walked back up to the ranch. I sat down in the gathering room and hung my head low when Coach Mo walked up to me and placed his hand on my shoulder. He said something that I still remember to this day. In that deep, bass voice he said, "Danny, some day you are gonna have to be okay with the choices you make." Then he removed his hand and walked away. It was as if I had been blindsided with the truth. My entire life flashed before my eyes. I regretted everything!

"Danny, some day you are gonna have to be okay with the choices you make."

I regretted getting fat; I regretted smoking; I regretted gambling; I regretting putting my family into debt; I regretted giving up on music; I regretted being a poor role model to my kids; I regretted *everything!* It seemed every decision I made was a poor decision. At this point in my life, I was almost too scared to make any decision at all. I frequently found myself standing at a fork in the road, worrying about which way to go. I would freeze in fear as my life passed me by and my journey was halted. Instead of choosing something and going with it, I would sit there contemplating the "what if's" and the "maybe's" and would waste valuable time. Opportunities would pass me by as I stood by like a deer in headlights, scared that whatever I did would be wrong. My life was a mess, and this mess had nothing to do with 430 pounds! But it had everything to do with a lack of confidence in myself to succeed at anything.

Well, the slap in the face with the truth by Coach Mo wasn't enough to wake me up. To top everything off, Tracey picked her team, and I wasn't on it. She threw me to the others like bait to a shark. She did, however, pick Liz. So Liz and I, who had been together since day one, were separated. *And,* Tracey threw me to Jillian Michaels, too. I didn't want Jillian Michaels! I hated the screaming and the beatings she gave! I wanted Bob Harper and the care he gave me! He made me feel safe. Well, with safety comes comfort, and you can hardly learn anything about life when you are comfortable!

Later that day, Jillian was beating me up in a workout. Now, if there's anything you *don't* want, it is Jillian beating you up in a

workout. She is *scary!* There's nothing nice about Jillian in the gym. If there were anyone I'd want as my bodyguard in a bar fight, it would be Jillian! She's only 5'2" tall and 115 pounds, but she is one tough cookie!

She asked me to sit down when she made me fail at a sprint, and I sat on the treadmill as she knelt beside me. She leaned over and put her hand on my shoulder and said, "Danny, there's something you have to learn. Every decision you make isn't going to be the best one. Right and wrong are such harsh terms! You have to take the good decisions you make and run with them. You take the bad decisions you make and you find the value in them; you learn from them. But if you regret your decisions, you'll never move forward in your life. If you get this concept, you'll go on to do great things. If you don't, you'll get stuck, going through the same cycle over and over again. Regrets just hold you back, Peanut!"

Yes, Jillian called me Peanut! How can you call a 380-pound man Peanut? This is Jillian Michaels we are talking about! Well, that day, a new light shone on a dark part of my life. When you expose the darkness to light, you can never hide in it again. I decided that I was going to stop letting my regrets hold me back from my destiny, and I found the value in eating that cupcake.

"You have to take the good decisions you make and you run with them. You take the bad decisions you make and you find the value in them; you learn from them. But if you regret your decisions, you'll never move forward in your life. Regrets just hold you back!"

Was I glad about playing that game and eating that cupcake? No way! But because I did, I became more focused and more determined than ever. I responded to my situation by working harder that week than any other week. I decided that since I had eaten those calories, I would simply work harder and longer than the others to work the calories off. So when I let go of the regret of making a poor decision and I decided to turn that energy into a positive force, everything changed. I never fell below the yellow line again, and when I weighed in that week the scale showed a double digit weight loss. We beat the "stacked" Blue Team and sent them into the elimination room. I was charged up and ready to go! And the double digit weight loss I had that week was the first of seven straight weeks, which is still a record on *The Biggest Loser* as of this writing!

I'm telling you now that if you follow your heart and begin to move, even the bad decisions you might make don't have to rule your life. How you respond is the important thing. You can take out your hammer and beat yourself up about it or you can decide to get back up and move forward in your life. Everything can bring value. Even being 460 pounds! People ask me every day, "If you could go back, would you change those 17 years of being obese?" Not a chance! I am who I am today because of where I came from. Although being 460 pounds was unhealthy and life-threatening, I can now see the value in being there. I can now show others that what was meant to harm them, even the bad decisions they have made, can be turned to achieve something good. Just as the scripture Genesis 50:20 says, "You intended to harm me, but God intended it for good to accomplish what is now being done, the saving of many lives."

I can now show, because of the path that I have taken, that no matter how dire the circumstances are, anyone can choose to respond differently and use their experiences to fuel the next step in their lives. There is always hope and always a way out of the wilderness that surrounds you. Debt, addiction, anger, resentment, anything that can have control over your life can be conquered and the tide can be turned. You just have to lose the regrets and decide to respond to your circumstances in a different, more productive way.

Lose the Lies

There was a time in my life when I was full of regrets. It seemed that my world had shrunk from endless possibility to sure failure. My kids were watching their 460-pound father struggle just to walk, not being able to tie his own shoes without holding his breath. I often wonder what went through their minds when I walked out to the pool and their friends were with them. I'm sure they were embarrassed.

There was a time when I volunteered for my children's school carnival. I was going to oversee the obstacle course! My kids went up to Darci and asked, "Where's Dad?" When she told them, they looked at her with sadness in their eyes. When Darci asked why they were upset they quietly answered, "Great. They're all going to make fun of him."

When my wife told me about that conversation later, I cried. I was an embarrassment to my children, a failure as a true provider, and anything but the hero I wanted to be for my family. When I looked in the mirror I didn't always notice the failure. But I was lying to myself about just where I was in my life. Let me go back to the beginning.

When I was in high school, I went to a concert. I never knew how to play guitar, and the ability seemed a mystery to me. But that night, I carefully watched the guitar player's hands as he played. I watched as his fingers danced around the fret board while he plucked the strings. While watching that night, I realized something. I saw the relation between space and time on that guitar. It all became possible to me!

After that revelation, I was motivated to learn! And it didn't hurt that I didn't have a girlfriend and there were hundreds of girls begging for the band's attention. But I looked a little deeper than most of us do. I searched for the secret to playing guitar and found that it was possible. I thought, If he can do it, I can do it! So I went home, borrowed (well, stole) my sister's guitar and began playing; one note at a time and one string at a time. I was going to figure this thing out.

I met a guitar player and he told me I was playing single lines and that was what the bass guitarist does, so I promptly went to the nearest pawn shop and looked around for a bass. I spent my hard-earned money on a hollow-body Epiphone bass guitar and

a s̶   ̶ok it home and went to work. And
yes,   *was* "Smoke on the Water." Wasn't it
eve̶

̶at practiced in Charlie's barn behind the school. When I went in to watch them rehearse, I watched them play and a fire grew in me that I couldn't control. Now the mechanism of being the best bass player in school appeared! My intention became clear and I was going to join this band! But how would I do it? Well, I asked if they played any other songs. The guitar player said, "Well, we want to play '*Detroit Rock City*,' but he can't play the bass part. We also want to play '*The Trooper*,' but the bass part is too difficult."

I boldly made a statement. I declared, "Those aren't that hard! Why, if I wanted to, I could learn them in a week." Then, at that moment, I heard the one thing that I needed to hear. I heard Robby say, "No you can't." Now, to me, "them's fightin' words!" I went home, pulled out the tape deck, and proceeded to wear myself out trying over and over and over again to learn the songs. It was tough, but I lost my quit until I did learn them! I got all the way through both of them without a mistake.

The next week I went to their rehearsal. When they were finished practicing, I said, "Hey! Let's play 'Detroit Rock City!'" They looked at me and laughed. I asked to borrow the bass and said, "Let's just give it a try!" Well, I played my very first song with a band that day. And then I played my second. And the current bass player had played his last.

Music was in my blood. It was a natural ability to me. I had a strange ability to hear things that most people just couldn't hear in a song. My senses were just locked in. Now that I look back, it all

makes sense. In the second grade I sang 'Country Roads' by John Denver, and I remember my music teacher always calling on me to sing the solos. I learned harmonica when I was 10; I just figured it out! And the same thing happened with the bass guitar. I sincerely felt that I had found my passion. Music became my love and land surveying became only my means to buy the equipment and pay for the studio time! My entire future had shifted by a single moment at a single concert. Over the next eleven years, I went from sitting in my room plucking a single guitar string to being a member of the group voted best band in Greece in 1996. Now, that was two years after things took a slight detour.

I had just finished playing a few jobs with a band named PC Quest, who at the time was in Billboard's Top 40. In fact, the last job I played with them was when we opened for the artist who had the number one single in the nation at the time! PC Quest replaced New Kids On The Block as the number one "kid" band and the ticket to my dreams was about to happen. But then, some plans of RCA Records changed and I was left behind to stay in Oklahoma while they all left for Los Angeles! My dreams were shattered - *again!* It wasn't like this was the first time it had happened. You see, this is when I reached the 99-yard line I was talking about earlier. I lost confidence in my musical abilities. I began seeing myself as a second-rate player and not the "I can do anything" musician that I was before. Well, just a short time later I tried one more time with a band named Unleash the Dog. But after a botched record deal with a label out of Utah, I decided enough was enough.

Again in my life, I had worked so hard and saw so little results. My quit crept in and I gave up on my dream. I asked my girlfriend to marry me and promptly quit the band. Darci was perplexed and asked, "Why are you quitting the band? You are so good! You love it!" But I was following that voice in my head that was telling me to quit. Remember, I hadn't lost my quit *or* my 239 pounds yet!

I couldn't combine my passion with my priorities.

Well, for years I had been told what it means to "be a provider" and "have obligations." My great uncle once said to me, "There's not a worker who's worth a damn until they have a family to support. Then they *have* to give it their all." So what I had been taught was that marriage and a music career didn't mix. I couldn't combine my passion with my priorities.

If I was going to get married, I had to "settle down." And immediately I heard that voice which tells us to *quit* and *give up* say, "Put away your pipe dream, boy. You're going to have to get a real job with a real income if you're going to be the provider for a family, just live like your father before you" and I immediately quit music. All of the passion in my heart succumbed to all of the negative thoughts that were in my head. That is how most dreams die, and mine wasn't any different – they die as we believe a lie we're told. My dreams got put up on a shelf and I turned my attention to every need but mine.

For the next 15 years, I focused on what everyone else thought I should be doing and turned my back on everything that I knew in my heart that I should be doing. My mother-in-law even called the Oklahoma State Board of Registration for Land Surveyors and Engineers and asked them to send her an application to take the Land Surveyors Licensing test. Now, Beverly didn't want to become a surveyor. She wanted *me* to become a surveyor. She then sent that application to me and forced the issue. Now, am I unhappy that I became a licensed surveyor? No way! But in doing what everyone else thought I should be doing and none of what I wanted to do, I lost my passion and I lost my lust for life.

My joy was gone, and I slowly transformed into an angry, unhappy man. All I could see was an endless series of work weeks where I walked through a door and did the monotonous job of land surveying every single day. Not that land surveying is monotonous, but because anything that you do that you don't wnat to do is monotonous. Especially since I moved into the confines of the office and left the beautiful countryside to the field crews I now managed. I completely lost my identity. In the movie *Return of the Jedi*, Luke Skywalker had many of the same gifts and traits of his father. At one point in the movie during a light saber battle with his father, he looks down to his hand; at his horror, it bore the very black glove that was his father's. I saw the same thing with my land surveyor's license and my Father's land surveyor license. It was as if I was in a chess game; I still had moves left in my dreams but I prematurely resigned the game!

Living life making the moves everyone else thinks you should make isn't much of a life at all. I lost all of the confidence in any abilities that I once had. As a result, I lost my identity. The once confident man that my wife met and fell in love with was now *half* the man at *twice* the size. When I gave up on my music, I gave up on me. Giving up didn't happen overnight. It happened day after day, decision after decision, and meal after meal. My lost dream of music slowly manifested for the world to see! My addiction could no longer be hidden like my gambling. After all, going from an extra-large shirt to a 6-X shirt is a pretty tough thing to hide.

But I was doing what I was supposed to be doing, right? Isn't that what you do when you love someone? Don't you put *their* needs above *your* needs? *Not necessarily.* I put myself as the last priority on the list with everyone else's needs on top of my own. It was like I was the very bottom face on the totem pole with the weight of everyone else's needs on my shoulders. After a while, that weight becomes unbearable.

*Isn't that what you do when you love someone?
Don't you put their needs above
your needs? Not necessarily.*

I spent nights hiding in video games, gambling, and eating. I was doing everything except what my passion was - writing songs. My instruments found their way under the bed and dust began to cover them. They cried out in silent screams, wanting to be played, but I refused to listen. I had *"other obligations"* and *"other priorities."* My needs would have to wait. The effect of what I was doing was not only taking its toll on me, but it was destroying my family. As a result of my ignoring my own needs, my family got the exact opposite of what they longed for.

Instead of the husband who could achieve anything, I became a shell of a man. When the head of a household becomes hard-hearted and angry, the home is in an uproar. My wife didn't know what to do. She married a confident musician and a few short years later, she found herself alone with a stranger in her house. She no longer knew me and I continued to grow more bitter by the day. My kids needed a father who showed them it was possible to achieve your dreams and that you could combine your passions with your priorities. Instead, they got a father who was angry and would begin an angry tirade at the smallest infraction! It seemed the only feedback they received was negative, and hope was dwindling in their lives, too.

To make matters even worse, I couldn't do anything with my family; I was physically too big! If we went to the zoo I would constantly have to sit down because my legs would hurt and ache. I couldn't ride any rides with them at the amusement park except the log ride. Darci became their riding partner while I watched from the sideline. And with each ride I missed, I became angrier with myself. When you stuff your anger it will eventually show up; and mine would be uncovered almost daily.

I once owned a 1951 GMC five-window pickup. It was my pride and joy! But there came a day when I couldn't even fit in the truck anymore. Instead of walking outside and having to look at the truck I could no longer drive, I sold it. I hate that I did, and it was another of the effects of my obesity that I have to live with. My kids were lost in a life where their father, their hero, was in a hurricane of self-hate and rage. This took its toll on them, as well as on my wife.

My obesity tended to feed itself. As I became bigger, I just threw up the white flag even more. What was the use of even trying to lose weight? I remember the day when I sat in my office and resigned myself to the fact that I would die an early death. The only thing that would make me feel more at ease was that my life insurance policy would at least pay off the house and debt. I was so relieved I got the term insurance *before* I gained all the weight because now, I wouldn't even qualify for insurance! My thoughts were turning more and more negative with each moment of each day.

Now, if you asked all my friends, they'd tell you I was still a happy guy! That is because I was living a lie in the *outside world*. It was amazing how much leeway I gave everyone outside my home. But as soon as I walked into my house, I let loose. The world saw a different Danny than my family did. They saw the Danny with a mask of serenity and fun. My family was my punching bag.

The lies I lived were all around me. I told myself lie after lie after lie. It was my coping mechanism - the way that I hid from myself the truth of what I really was. I used to tell myself I wasn't really that big. I used to look in the mirror and say to myself, "Well, I'm big, but I'm healthy!" Can you imagine a 460-pound man thinking he is healthy?!

I literally imagined running out into oncoming traffic. How much easier would everyone's life be if I just did that?

There was nothing healthy about me except my appetite! I used to say I was naturally a big guy. I was "big boned" and a "meat and potatoes" man. I never went shopping. If I did, I was reminded just how few places even carried clothes my size! My wife would go buy the clothes herself. It was a nightmare. When I did go shopping and the button-down shirts were all too small, I would get angry and depressed. I remember leaving the Big and Tall store and looking at the traffic in the street. I literally imagined running out into oncoming traffic. How much easier would everyone's life be if I just did that? I never remembered thoughts like that until after the show was over. I actually thought everyone's life would be easier if I would just hurry up and die.

I never went to the doctor. If I did, he would make me get on the scale and I'd have to see just how big I really was! The largest documented weight I can remember was 458 pounds. I was so embarrassed. I could tell the nurse was thinking "Wow!" I would avoid the doctor or anything else that would make me have to weigh myself. Every time I stepped on the scale, I was told the truth about myself, and sometimes the truth hurts!

I remember sitting in the recliner one day and looking down at my leg. There was a sore on it and water was oozing out of my leg! I didn't know what it was! I touched the water and smelled it. I thought something was dripping from the ceiling! A few days later, my leg was red hot! We went to the minor emergency and they told me I had an infection in my leg; that edema was causing it. They gave me antibiotics and sent me on my way. I never knew that it was a result of my morbid obesity until later! And if I had known, I would have probably denied it.

There was a time when I began sleeping in the living room in the recliner. I couldn't lie flat on my back and breathe! My back would ache and it was just easier to sleep sitting up. When I'd fall asleep sitting up from my exhaustion because of my severe sleep apnea, it just made it easier! My wife slept in the bed without a husband for years. For years I slept in a recliner, telling myself it was because of a bad back. I just wouldn't own up to the truth of being a severely morbidly obese man! I just kept telling myself lies.

Once, my wife and I were eating in our favorite Chinese food restaurant. When I looked through the restaurant, I saw an obese man trying to get out of his chair. He was struggling so hard to get up that I remember thinking to myself, *Wow, that guy is huge!* I actually felt sorry for the man. I remember seeing him limping by with a bad knee and thinking that if he lost some weight it would be good for his legs. After he walked by, I leaned over and asked my wife, "How big am I compared to that guy?" You should have seen the look on her face. It was a blank stare with a hint of panic. After a moment, she leaned over and quietly said, "You're a little bigger than he is, honey."

I was devastated. So devastated in fact that I laid my head down on the table and I cried. That was the first time I realized that I was lying to myself about just how obese I really was! We all tend to do that. We wear those "rose-colored glasses" that hide the truth from us. We do it in relationships, addictions, and I did in my obesity.

Later, I was moving my parents from the house where I grew up to a 5-acre tract of land. My father had Chronic Obstructive Pulmonary Disease and they were going to move to the country and live the remaining days of his life the way he had always dreamed. We had only one more load to go. I pulled the truck up to the house and saw a group of people in the driveway. I remember thinking to myself, *What is going on here?! They should be boxing up the rest of the things.* When I walked up I noticed the entire family was there - my mother and father, sisters, wife and kids, and even the neighbor, Helga, from across the street. I asked what was going on and they said it was an intervention. I asked, "Who's it for?" I was trying to think of who could be on drugs and who needed an intervention.

That is when my father spoke up. "Danny," he said, "We are afraid we are going to lose you. You are getting so big that it is time you did something about it." My parents were afraid they might lose their own son. My wife and kids were just waiting until they would get the call that I had died. My wife used to wake up multiple times each night and place her hand on my chest just to make sure I was still alive. And there I stood, still believing the lies I was telling myself.

I was shocked. They asked me what I needed from them to lose the weight. My parents even offered to pay for Lap-Band surgery. They said it was time to do something now before it was too late. I told them there was *no need for those drastic measures.* I promised them I would do something about it and they didn't need to pay for the surgery. I lied - again!

Short Cuts Don't Work

I can tell you that surgery has worked for some, but if I had gone the surgery route, it wouldn't have worked. I would have gained back all the weight and then some. With me, short cuts don't work. If I was going to change my life, I was going to have to move the mountain myself. It couldn't be done with surgery. I'll tell you how I know this.

Back when I was gambling, I found myself $16,700 in credit card debt. We could barely make ends meet and pay the bills! My parents came to Broken Arrow to visit and we began talking about finances. I revealed that the credit-card debt was killing us and my mother and father became quite angry. They said there was no reason I should be paying the banks all that interest! My mother pulled out her checkbook and asked, "How much is it?" I was embarrassed, but at the same time relieved. I told her and she wrote out the check. She told me I could pay her back whenever I could and not to worry about the interest. I reluctantly but exitedly took her check and paid off all that debt. It was such a relief.

A few years later, I gathered up all my bills. The gambling had continued and I added up the debt. Well, I was $30,000 in credit-card debt *AND* I owed my parents $16,700! Oh my goodness! I had patched the wound and not dealt with the infection of my lack of self-discipline. It was going to take more than a short cut to solve my problems. That loan from my parents was just a temporary solution leading to an inevitable outcome. I was going to have to lose the lies and deal with the problem. Before that would happen, I would find myself over $45,000 in credit-card debt and owing my parents the $16,700. I first had to lose the lies about my debt, and that happened when I went to church.

You see, my father, my friends and my counsel were all telling me I should file for bankruptcy. Somehow, I just didn't feel it was right. I did, however, let my wife talk to the attorney about it. He told her I would have to shut my business down, quit paying all bills except my house payment and car loans, and default on everything. Although not a single person was telling me to do differently, I felt in my heart that I was not supposed to do this. I just couldn't walk away from the mess I had made. That's just not the type of person I am. I prayed to God with my wife to give us a word on what to do. We were in a desperate situation and needed help.

"The only way out is through."

We went to church that night and Joyce Meyer had come to teach. She said, "I am going to start you out with a statement. The only way out is through." I looked at Darci and she looked at me, and I was relieved. Darci was scared, but we knew we had heard what we had gone to hear. I became committed to paying off every cent of that debt. We went home and pulled out all the paperwork. We entered a debt-reduction program and cut up our credit cards and began our long, tough journey to freedom. We knew it wouldn't be easy, but we knew it was right. And four years later, we paid our last payment to the credit cards and became debt-free except for our house and my parents. That day was a triumphant day! And it set the tone for the rest of my life.

When I lost the lies, I found my strength

You see, if I hadn't lost the lies and worked my way out of debt I would have never had the confidence to take each of the millions of steps on *The Biggest Loser* to win the show. It all happened for a reason and when I lost the lies, I found my strength. With commitment and focus, I regained the confidence that I could do anything I set my mind to; nothing would be impossible again. All I had to do was lose the lies and *decide* to do it. But until I admitted where I was, I couldn't begin to go where I wanted. In any journey, there are two things you need to know—your location and your destination. The path will appear when your destination and intention become clear.

My partner on the show, Liz Young, was in the same boat I was with her weight. She used to get her clothes out of the dryer and go to her husband holding them up. "Look! The dryer shrunk

my shirt! The dryer shrunk my pants! There's something wrong with our dryer! It is shrinking all my clothes!" I wonder why his clothes stayed the same while hers shrunk smaller and smaller? Look, the dryer wasn't broken. And it wasn't a special dryer that only shrunk her clothes! Like me, she was growing out of her clothes but refused to lose the lies and see the truth for what it was. It was easier to blame the dryer than face the issues that were making her eat. The lies we tell ourselves keep us in the same place that we don't want to be.

Have you ever believed the lies? I would venture to say you have. Have you ever wanted to get healthy and said, "I'll start Monday" right before you take a bite out of your *last* double cheeseburger? Or maybe you've wanted to go back to school to get that degree only to say, "I can't go back to school! I'm too old!" And we all have believed the biggest lie we tell ourselves at one time or another. That lie is, "I don't have enough time." I sure used that one a lot! And I still catch myself in that lie!

When I was working 16-hour days to pay off all that debt, I used to tell myself, "I don't have the time to work out." That was my excuse to sit on my butt and gain more weight! It was a lie that was ruling my life! And I have to be honest with you. When you took a quick glance at my life it *did* look like I didn't have enough time. But if you looked a little closer, the time was there. I just didn't make it a priority! There were times I spent a few minutes on Facebook or YouTube instead of working. There was time I spent watching television and putting my feet up to rest in my chair after a long day's work. Those minutes could have been spent doing something else if I'd only put losing the weight higher on my priority list! But I believed the lie that I didn't have enough time so I never lost the weight.

***You never have enough time to do anything.
You must make the time.***

You never *have* enough time to do anything. You must *make* the time. Time is precious, and people even use that as an excuse to let themselves go. One of my friends who lost a lot of weight has gained back much of what he lost. I, too, have gained about 25 pounds since my father passed away recently. I think we could encourage each other to lose the weight by working out together. When I asked him to come by on his way to or from work and exercise with me he said, "Well, we only have one car and with my wife and kids penned up in the house all day, I really need to get home." I replied that they might need him to be healthy more than they need those 45 minutes with him right now. But he, too, is believeing the lies.

And I know what he's going through because I used to do the same thing.

I also find myself relying on lies to help me avoid those things that are frightening or what I really need to do but don't want to do. Discipline is doing what needs to be done, even when it doesn't feel good to do it. To have discipline, one must lose the lies.

Find Your "Why"

After *The Biggest Loser* was over and I was the reigning champion, I was asked to join Jillian Michaels for interviews to promote the new and upcoming season of *The Biggest Loser*. After over a dozen interviews, Jillian turned to me and said, "If you find your *why* you can tolerate any *how*." Later that evening, I thought about that profound statement a lot. She was right. The reason I even tried out for *The Biggest Loser* in the first place was because I had found my *WHY*.

"If you find your WHY
you can tolerate any HOW."

When I was very young, I didn't have any sign of a weight problem. Then, suddenly at the age of seven, I gained weight and was on the way to becoming an obese child. This was between my 2nd and 3rd grade year. I'm not completely sure why I gained the weight, but it came on pretty quickly. Perhaps it was because we had just moved schools and I felt like an outsider to everyone. Maybe it was because I longed for the approval of others and that was a time when that approval didn't come. Whatever the reason, it wasn't easy; in fact, it was terribly hard. In the third grade, you begin finding your way in society. Thoser questions had begun to be asked about everyone in our class. "Who's the smartest kid in the class?" "Who's the cutest kid in the class?" "Who's the nicest kid in the class?" "Who's the most popular kid in the class?"

Well, imagine how I felt when the question was asked, "Who's the fattest kid in the class?" And the answer was *ME!* It was definitely no cakewalk. In fact, it was horrific! There was a time in grade school when we were learning country music dancing and we were practicing. When we paired up in partners for the dance, the girl who was chosen for me said, "Ewwww! I don't want to dance with Danny! I already showered today!" You see, overweight people sweat considerably more than in-shape people, and I had been sweating up a storm. That one moment devastated me. I was so embarrassed.

Well, I was overweight throughout school and often didn't have a girlfriend. But it became extra hard for me in junior high school. The kids were "pairing up" and getting girlfriends, and I hadn't had a girlfriend in quite a while. I felt like an outcast. All of my friends had girlfriends, and I wanted one too! My sophomore year was perhaps the hardest year of my childhood. I was 250 pounds and I was the farthest thing from any girl's mind except when they wanted to laugh. When I left at the end of the year, I was finished. I went home and said, "THAT'S IT!" I was bound and determined to get that girlfriend! So I left school for summer vacation and began a regimine. I would run three miles every day and eat nothing but salads and drink diet pop to keep myself full!

Yes, it was pretty much starvation and exercise. I would never recommend anyone to lose weight that way, but I did it. When I drove to enroll in school my junior year, I weighed a firm 175 pounds! I had lost 75 pounds that summer!

I heard the girls whispering, "Is that Danny Cahill?! WOW! I can't believe how good he looks!" Needless to say, I did get my girlfriend that year! And do you know why I got the girl that year? Because I had *found my WHY!*

You see, when losing the weight became my deepest intent, the *HOW* to lose weight appeared! And nothing was too hard. I was able to tolerate anything needed to get the job done. When I found my "WHY," I found my *discipline.* But before I had that reason why, anything that had to do with losing weight was just torture. I had to define the reason that would make all of the work and self-control worth it. Once I defined it and the why was bigger than the excuses, the results appeared.

When I found my "WHY," I found my discipline.
But before I had that reason why,
anything that had to do with
losing weight was just torture.

Now, you might be asking yourself, "What was Danny's why to become The Biggest Loser?" That's very hard for me to talk about without getting emotional, but it must be talked about for you to fully understand what happened.

My daughter, Mary Claire, was seven years old. I was 458 pounds at the time and spent much of my time sitting. As I told you before, a simple thing like getting up and walking a few steps was terrible! The television was on and Mary came in the room. I remember looking at her and noticing that she had gained weight. My heart sank as I thought to myself, *Please, God. Don't make her go through what I went through! I pray she doesn't have a weight problem!*

Well, she walked right up to me, put her around me and she said, "Daddy, You're my hero!" At that point my heart swelled with pride! I was so glad that my little girl wanted to be just like me! But then she continued, "I want a belly just like yours!" It felt like my heart fell into my stomach. You see, at that point I had a 69" waist!

I promptly said, "No, you don't!" To which she replied, "Yes, I do!" This went on for a while until I finally figured out that I would never win this argument with a seven-year old girl like Mary Claire! I was stunned. Well, I promptly got up off of the couch, which was a really big deal, and walked into the bathroom. I looked at myself in the mirror - into the dark part of my eyes - and I said, "What is wrong with you? This isn't just you at stake! It's your whole family!" And a tear ran down my face.

I made a decision that day in 2008 that I would do something about my weight. I'd tried a thousand times to lose weight and failed, but this time it would be different! I didn't know then that I would soon set the goal of getting on *The Biggest Loser* and losing the most weight in the history of the show…but that is precisely what I did!

I wasn't sure exactly what I was going to do, but my wife was going through a severe depression at the time. I'm sure it didn't have *anything* to do with the fact that I was a few pounds over-weight and she feared she would lose me to it soon. She went through a seminar in Dallas, Texas, which helped pull her out of her depression. She came home and promptly begged me to go. Of course, I replied, "That's great that it helped you, but I'm fine! I don't need any seminar!"

Well, I finally decided to go a few months later and boy had I been wrong! I went with a purpose; to change my life. When you purpose in your heart to change and you find a *WHY* as big as my Mary Claire, the limits are completely lifted! In the second part of the seminar, we were talking about dreams and goals. When asked to share what your dream and goal was, I stood and said something amazing. I said, "I am going to get on *The Biggest Loser* and win the show. I want to lose more weight than anyone else in the history of the show!" The people just looked at me in amazement. I might as well have said I wanted to jump over the moon! To them, it sounded the same. But to me, it sounded possible.

I wrote it down in my journal and decided that was going to be the vehicle I used to right my life and write a new story! Now, there are thousands of ways to lose weight, but this one might have been the most outrageous I could think of!

Out of over 300,000 entrants for Season 8, I not only made it to the show (which was a miracle in itself,) but I won the show and became The Biggest Loser ever by losing 56% of my body weight! I actually reached that goal I had set for myself over a year before! But I never would have done it had I not found my *WHY*. And it wouldn't have happened had my *WHY* not been big enough to drive me through the disappointments and the pain. I can say this because I tried out for Season 6 of *The Biggest Loser,* five different times for Season 7, and finished with getting on Season 8. If you knew what it took to try out for that show, you'd definitely realize that just not giving up on that was a task!

I finally figured out that my weight was ruining not only my life, but also my family's lives. It was weighing everyone down and there was no one to blame except me. The simple realization of that - admitting I had a problem and that I was the problem - was the first step in healing what was wrong. *The Biggest Loser* was the vehicle for the weight loss, but I can honestly say that with or without it, I believe that I was ready to make the change. I had definitely defined the reason *WHY* in my life—my family.

The time that my family had an intervention with me, it didn't have a chance of working. The reason I say that is that my *WHY* had to come from inside of me. It couldn't be from my family. It had to come from my heart. I had to feel it, define it, and want it for myself, and no intervention could possibly give that to me. Quite frankly, had I listened and had the surgery and lost the weight at that point, I'd have gained it all back. I wasn't ready to change.

Before I quit smoking, my best friend David, my in-laws, and my friends would tell me they wished I would quit. But I never would. It had to be that day that I'd had enough. I remember sitting at the stop light and getting so mad that I held up a cigarette and began to yell at it. I said, "You don't control me! I've had it up to HERE with you! I've had enough! I can't take this anymore! How can this little thing control my entire life?" I was actually having an argument with a cigarette! It may sound weird to you, but it must have really looked weird to the guy in the car next to me at the stop light! He looked stunned. I went to my church that night and prayed with someone, crumpled up my pack of cigarettes, and threw them across the room! I found my *WHY*! I went palms up and was ready for it to end! I never smoked again, and never even had a withdrawal symptom! I was done!

When Darci and I tackled the *how* of getting out of debt, we sat at the table and were at the end of our rope. I am a very loyal and honest man, and I felt like I was cutting corners and leaving my debt for someone else to cover if we filed for bankruptcy. We didn't know what to do. That night when we went to church and Joyce Meyer was there and we heard what she said to us, we found our *WHY*. We would no longer choose to run from the problem anymore and instead we chose to become a master of our finances instead of being mastered by our finances. When it became our deepest intent to take care of the debt, we found the way to tolerate the work, discipline, and self-control needed to do it!

External motivation is great, but if that's all you have, it won't take you far. Without a clearly defined *WHY*, it will be too easy to lean on the same excuses that have kept you where you've been for far too long. Zig Ziglar once said, "People often say motivation doesn't last. Well, neither does bathing - that's why we recommend it daily." And I can tell you that the best way to motivate every day is to define your *WHY*, remind yourself of your *WHY* every day, and make it the main source of your motivation.

External motivation is great, but if that's all you have it won't take you far. Without a clearly defined WHY, it will be too easy to lean on the same excuses that have kept you where you've been for too long.

If you're waiting for some external motivation to get you moving forward, you'll be waiting forever. If you're looking for a validation of the decisions you make, don't bother; it wouldn't matter anyway. And if you are looking for some amazing event to move you into your destiny, it's not going to happen. Your *WHY* has to come from inside of you and from no external source.

I've been asked, "How do you know when you've found your true *WHY?*" Well, it is simply when you can tolerate *any* how. Your situation won't matter. Your finances won't matter. And setbacks won't matter, either! Setbacks are always going to happen. But when you have found your true *WHY,* you can come back twice as strong as before. Look at it like walking up a set of stairs and slipping on a step. You have to have the purpose to begin climbing again. That is the only way you will ever reach the top.

I knew I had found my true *WHY* because I could clearly visualize my goal. I actually saw myself as a thinner, fitter man! I saw myself standing in front of my daughter and my family and inspiring them instead of worrying them. I also saw myself standing on the scale and winning *The Biggest Loser;* confetti in my hair and Alison Sweeney saying those words. "You are the Biggest Loser, Danny!"

On *The Biggest Loser*, my first big setback was 6' 4" and wearing blue. His name was Rudy. When I got to the ranch and we went to that first weigh-in, I weighed 12 pounds less than Rudy. Four weeks into the competition, Rudy weighed five pounds less than I did. All I could see was the goal of being the Biggest Loser being pushed farther and farther away from me! But I soon found my stride by not giving up and I eventually surpassed Rudy and never looked back. My *WHY* fueled my engine and nothing was going to stop me. That is what one needs to achieve any goal they set. They need a *WHY* so big that the goal is their first priority and when hurdles come, they jump over them! Finding your *WHY* is the only way to ensure you won't lose your footing on the way up that mountain you have to climb.

The Time Is Now

So let's recap. You've got to:

- *Lose Your Quit*
- *Lose Your Regrets*
- *Lose the Lies*
- *Find Your Why*

These four steps can move you so far forward in your life that you will be able to accomplish things you never thought possible. During *The Biggest Loser* Season 10, Ali Ishcomer, a contestant from Moore, Oklahoma, was the first person who left the show. I went to see her and gave her some advice. I told her that she had to quit relying on everyone around her to tell her she could do it and she had to begin believing it herself. Now, don't get me wrong - we need positive people around us who support our goals and dreams, but there is only one person who is with us 100% of the time - ourselves. We have got to be the biggest support structure we have. Without the belief in ourselves and our goals and dreams, we are doomed to fail.

---

*Great dreams and world-changing ideas
die with the people who don't act on them.*

Now that you've taken the first four steps, let's talk about the fifth step. It is time for you to take action! Great dreams and world-changing ideas die with the people who don't act on them. Any invention that has changed the world - the car, the telephone, the airplane, and many others - would have never been invented had someone not acted on an idea. Every great thing begins with a simple idea. It might be, "How can I clean my wood floors more efficiently?" It might be, "Someone should do something about that." It might be, "How can I lose this weight?"

My good friend and mentor, Jim Stovall - author of the award winning movie *The Ultimate Gift* and of the movie *A Christmas Snow* as well as world-class motivational speaker - did this very thing. Jim went blind at a time in his life when things looked so promising for him. He was devastated. At a certain point, he put on a movie he had seen before. For a while he remembered all of the scenes even though he couldn't see them, but then something happened. The movie reached a point where he didn't remember exactly what happened. He became so angry. He thought to himself, "Someone ought to do something about that." At that moment, Narrative Television Network was born. He had the idea of narrating television shows and movies for the blind and visually impaired. This means a lot to me, because my wife's grandmother, Elenora Jackson, also known as GG, had macular degeneration.

She could never see the television. I remember, before I met Jim and knew about NTN, thinking the same thing. Well, Jim did something about it! He was told by naysayers that he couldn't do it, but he was determined. Now, he has changed the way that the visually impaired "watch" television and movies. He has changed the world. He didn't do it by coming up with a great idea. People come up with great ideas every day! He did it by acting on that great idea. So…are *you* going to act on your dreams? Are you going to act on your goals? Are you going to change your world?

Well, the answer completely depends on you. Right now, you could finish reading this book and go back to the same life that you were leading. You have the power to choose. Today I beg you; CHOOSE DIFFERENTLY! You can choose your destiny and stop letting your circumstances choose for you! And it starts right now. If you can't think of a way to act, I will give you a few in the last part of this chapter. Again, you could read this and then decide not to act, but my hope is that you are ready to stop "getting by" and start moving forward in your life.

Statistics show that only 3% of all people write down their goals. Statistics also show that the other 97% of society usually work for those 3%!

The first thing you can do is ***write down your goals.*** This is essential. Statistics show that only 3% of all people write down their goals. Statistics also show that the other 97% of society usually work for those 3%! Being an "odds" guy, I think I'll take those odds! Do you want to achieve your goals and dreams? If you do, write them down. Place them on your mirror. Place them in your car. Hang them in your office. Make it so you can't avoid seeing that goal staring you in the face, begging you "achieve me!"

When I was speaking at an event in Las Vegas, another speaker was Billy Blanks – the creator of Tae Bo, an aerobic routine that has sold several million copies worldwide. After my speech, I sat quietly in the back of the auditorium and watched Billy. This guy is intense! I mean, he looks as if he could jump through the roof at any moment! But one thing he had us do was incredible. He said, "When I say go, begin counting silently in your head. Then, when I speak, repeat the word I say." We all began counting in our head. He then said, "Bingo!" We all repeated, "Bingo!" Just when I was wondering why in the heck he had us do this, he spoke up. He asked, "What happened to your counting?" Someone said, "It stopped." He screamed, *"EXACTLY!"*

He told us something amazing. He said that it is extremely hard for your mind to think on something other than what your mouth is speaking. What this told me was that when you speak something out of your mouth, your brain is forced to hear it and think on it. After reaffirming your goals and dreams, your mind eventually begins to believe it. It can't help it!

So when you want to achieve something, begin speaking it out. In the Bible, it says in Proverbs 18:21 that the tongue holds the power of life and death. I completely believe this. It holds the power of life and death in your dreams. It holds the power of life and death in your children. It is a very powerful weapon. But it can be used *for* or *against* your goals and dreams. Here's a perfect example.

On *The Biggest Loser*, I was at the ranch for 12 weeks. My wife was at home with the bills and the kids. She had so much pressure on her. On top of that, she felt that she should lose weight right along with me to support me. She lost a whopping 47 pounds while I was away for those first three months! Not only this, but a few weeks before I got home, she began to run. Now, this might not seem like such a big deal, but it is. You see, Darci absolutely *hates* running. She has loathed it since she was a child! The thought of it made her want to die! But for some reason, she began telling herself, "I am a runner! I am a runner!" And before I got home, she could run a few miles without stopping.

The great thing about this story is that just after I returned home, I received a call from Jillian Michaels. She told me we were about to do something we had never done before. When I asked what it was, she replied, "You're going to run a marathon." I gasped! Darci gasped! We were shocked! It was crazy! Just three months before, I was 430 pounds and Darci was 217 pounds. Now, in 60 days I was going to run a marathon? Then, about 30 days after that call something amazing happened.

Darci received a call and was asked if she could run the last half of the marathon with me. It was 13.1 miles! Well, she did it. The girl who hated running had convinced herself that she *was* a runner and as a result, she ran a half-marathon with just a few months of training!

So, as Henry Ford said, "Whether you think you can, or you think you can't - you're right." Are you going to speak words of life and positive affirmations from your mouth or will you speak death and negative thoughts about your goals? I have to say that at 458 pounds, I spoke negatively about my goals. I used to say the mountain was too high to climb. After all, if I lost 100 pounds, I would still have over 150 to go! How would you feel with that size of a job to do? Something tells me there is an area in life that you think *exactly* that. But I know that you have it in you to do whatever you set your mind to.

Well, the day I wrote my goal down, that I would get on and win *The Biggest Loser*, all that negativity changed. And less than a year later, I was leaving for the ranch. Less than 7 months after that, I had lost 55.58% of my body weight and was crowned the Biggest Loser EVER in the history of the show. I spoke positive thoughts and daily affirmations every time I rose from bed. I read positive scriptures and thoughts from the basket that my mother-in-law Beverly had given me. I posted my goal of "180 pounds" everywhere! It was my password on my BodyBugg account! It was on my wrist. It was what I told everyone around me.

For two weeks before Thanksgiving, I worked out eight hours every single day and only lost eight pounds. I hit 195 pounds twelve days before the final weigh-in for the show. I realized that I had lost just about every bit of fat on my body! I lost an additional four pounds to weigh in at 191 and beat Rudy by 14 pounds to win the title. I set a lofty goal, knowing if I had the weight to lose, I could achieve it. Who can argue that I did all I could and laid it all out on the table. I went all in and won the world series of weight loss - The Biggest Loser! I held absolutely nothing back. And it began with speaking it out of my mouth!

Another thing you can do to start is to make yourself accountable to someone. Yes, you must be accountable to yourself, but it helps to have others in your life to be accountable to. I told my goals to my wife. Every morning she would almost push me out the door to exercise. Every night she would ask me if I achieved my daily calorie-burn goal. It almost became irritating! But accountability is what I needed.

> *You must be accountable to yourself,*
> *but it helps to have others in your life*
> *to be accountable to.*

I made myself accountable to my great friend, Arthur Greeno. Arthur is an owner of two Chick-fil-A locations in the Tulsa, Oklahoma, area. That in itself is amazing. Less than 13% of all Chick-fil-A owners operate more than a single location. What inspires me about Arthur is that he is action-oriented. Most people ask, "Could we really do this?" Arthur asks, "Why not? Let's go!" Because of that, he has set two Guinness World Records for the

largest hand-squeezed lemonade (840 Gallons) and the largest iced
tea (1,140 Gallons in a 9-foot tall cup!)

Well, I tend to be an analyst. I tend to want to have all the
information before I act.
Sometimes, you miss
opportunity that way.
Arthur might fall a lot,
but he succeeds a lot, too!
That is what I needed.
So, when he asked how
he could help me, I asked him to hold my feet to the fire a bit.
Well, he promptly joined my gym. We didn't get to work out much
together there, but we did a few times. When I finished working
out one evening, Arthur came by and asked, "Have you got your
burn?" The gym was closing down and I said, "No. I'm going to
miss it a bit tonight. I'll make up for it tomorrow." Now I was only
going to be about 350 calories shy of making it, but Arthur just
wouldn't have it.

"Come on," he said. "There's a trail right down the road here."
And off we went. We walked until almost midnight that night,
and I got my burn! I left my phone in the car, so Darci finally
called Arthur and asked if he knew where I was. Arthur said, "He's
right here walking beside me. He's getting his burn." Now, I could
have told my goals to a friend who wouldn't have held my feet to
the fire, but that gets you nowhere. A friend like Arthur is who you
need beside you to succeed. A good friend doesn't let you make

decisions that are detrimental to your life. They call you when they think you might be giving in.

Another accountability partner was my daughter, Mary Claire. One morning I was answering emails on the computer. Darci said, "You need to get going! Go exercise!" I replied, "Leave me alone! I have to do this and I am tired." Mary quietly came up to me, put her hand gently on my shoulder and said, "Daddy, they gave you a second chance, but you won't get a third." I closed my eyes, breathed in deep, and got up out of that chair. That chair and that computer were two of the things that helped me get up to 458 pounds. It was time to re-prioritize my day and go get my dream! Thank God for little kids; they see things in such a simple way sometimes.

So if you want to be successful in your goals, find someone who will hold you accountable to them and ask them to help. Yeah, I know - you really don't want to do that. Well, neither did I, but doing so got me to my goal. So if hiding and not being accountable is more important to you than succeeding, don't get an accountability partner or group. But if your deepest commitment is to succeed, pick up the phone right now and make a few calls. Don't even wait until you finish this chapter. Do it now!

"Do a little more today than yesterday;
repeat that process tomorrow."

If you do the same things you've always done, you'll get the same results. I always say, "Do a little more today than yesterday; repeat that process tomorrow." Pick something you haven't done before and just do it! When I went to the ranch, I obviously began an intense exercise regimen. When you have Jillian Michaels and Bob Harper as trainers, they make you do more than you've ever done before! But what most people don't know is that we have an unlimited amount of food to eat. They stock huge refrigerators and freezers with an immense amount of food. We can eat all we want! And some did eat more than others. They often lost much less than those who did something different than they had done before! Every day, I had to answer the question - would I do what I'd always done or do something different and keep a strict log of my calories? I chose differently, and stuck to it the entire show - and I succeeded.

So if you do what you did yesterday, you will stay in the same place you are. If you do a little more, you'll advance further on the path to your goals and dreams. And the amount you do is directly proportionate to how far you advance. The choice is yours!

Although there are things you need to add to your daily routine to succeed, there are also things you need to subtract. One thing you need to subtract is the naysayers! When I was trying out for the show, one of my very best friends in the world came down hard on me. He said, "I've had it with this pipe dream of getting on *The Biggest Loser!* Just do it now!" Well, my deepest commitment was to use *The Biggest Loser* as one of the tools to not only lose the weight, but also to change other's lives. So I quit talking to him altogether. I decided to remove all the negativity being spoken into my life and add only the positive people. It worked! I kept moving towards my goal for three seasons until I made it to Season 8! Since then, my friend and I talk often, and now I believe my Biggest Loser journey has even affected his life!

This brings to mind another story that happened about a year after I finished *The Biggest Loser*. A friend of mine was diagnosed with cancer. It was progressing and I have to say that he did look terrible one day when I saw him at church. He came up to me and said, "I'm going to train for a triathlon." My first thought was, *Are you nuts?* But then I remembered something important; I remembered that I lost 239 pounds in less than seven months! Why couldn't he do a triathlon? I removed the limits of cancer and said to him, "Be careful, but go for it!"

Well, he began his training and immediately came the naysayers. First, his wife came up to me and asked me to talk him out of it! Now, you have to understand that she thought she had his best interests at heart. She told me that the doctor said it would kill him to do this. I did ask my friend if the doctor had said negative things about his training. He told me his doctor actually resigned from treating him. His doctor said, "I cannot condone this and I will not be a part of this insanity." His doctor thought it was in his best interest not to do this.

Well, my friend decided to go on with his training and finish the triathlon despite the naysayers. One day after the race, he began having chest pains. He drove himself to the hospital and they admitted him. They ended up placing a stint in his artery. When the cardiologist came in, my friend asked him, "Did this happen because of my triathlon training?" He told my friend, "Sir, I am absolutely positive that if you hadn't been training for that triathlon, you'd be dead right now." The doctor went on to say that the training strengthened his heart enough to allow him to survive the heart attack that was going to happen with or without the training.

So what others said would kill him actually saved his life. What is so great about that is before I went to *The Biggest Loser*, while sitting in my surveying office, I needed encouragement. Sometimes when I need encouragement, I just open my Bible and begin to read. Just one week before I received the call saying I was on the show, I opened to Genesis 50:20 which says, "You intended to harm me, but God intended it for good to accomplish what is now being done, the saving of many lives." That scripture gave me hope that I was going to get on *The Biggest Loser* and that it would change other's lives, too! For my friend it meant this - that from which others try to deter you might actually save your life. Had he listened to the naysayers, he might very well have died.

When you know in your heart that you are supposed to do something, *just do it*. I am not telling you to ignore doctor's orders or leave your loved ones, but I am telling you to follow your heart.

I'm telling you to refuse to believe the lies and even if you have to get a second opinion, *just do it!*

So what one thing can you do when you put this book down to change the direction of your physical future? I can honestly tell you that you do not need a reality show to change your life. You simply need to change your mind and decide differently. You need to Lose Your Quit, Lose Your Regrets, Lose the Lies, and Find Your Why. Then you need to Lose the Later and ACT NOW - the sooner the better. If you are waiting to start tomorrow, please realize that tomorrow never comes! You must begin today!

The only limits you have are the ones you place on yourself, so why limit yourself? Today is your second chance at life, so take it now! I'm going to end this book with the lyrics to my song, "Second Chance." It was the song I wrote on The Biggest Loser Ranch and was inspired by my journey to change my life. I think the lyrics can be used to inspire you to change your life in whatever you want to do. After all, it is all about taking your second chance at life, and the beginning of that new life can be today!

Second Chance

Just a dream put on a shelf; just a thought you put away; but you were lying to yourself; living day to day.

Take your heart and wake it up; get yourself back in the race; go and win the silver cup; show the world your face.

You can do it, there ain't nothing to it; all you need is to get yourself back!

This is your Second Chance at life, don't you wait there for it; this is your Second Chance at life, you are ready for it! You hold your future in your hands and all you've got to do is run! Run this race with all your heart; and take your second chance.

You always had it in yourself; it was right there all along; but then you lost your way; and then you lost your song. But it's never too late to get yourself back on your horse; and write some brand new words; learn to stay the course.

You can do it, there ain't nothing to it; all you need is to get yourself back!

This is your Second Chance at life, don't you wait there for it; this is your Second Chance at life, you are ready for it! You hold your future in your hands and all you've got to do is run! Run this race with all your heart; and take your second chance.

Now, in the words my father wrote to my son, "Go and get your dream, boy!"

LOSE YOUR QUIT

If you'd like motivation, go to www.LoseYourQuit.com and read my motivational blogs, and go to www.thedannycahill.com to purchase resources to help you along the path of your journey!

Also, like me on Facebook at www.facebook.com/thedannycahill and let me know how you are doing! I read all the posts and hope to answer any questions I can. If you'd like to hire me to speak at your company, church or event, please email me at danny@thedannycahill.com. Or just shoot me an email and ask any question you want! I do answer all emails. You can also follow me on Twitter at *@dannycahill1*.

I also spend some of my time volunteering for an organization whose goal is to launch people into their goals and dreams by helping them remove the limits they have placed on themselves. It is called The Journey Training (www.thejourneytraining.com). If you are interested in finding out more information on The Journey Training, email me and I will tell you all about it.

Don't wait to begin achieving your goals. Take a step and enjoy the journey to your dreams! And when you arrive, begin again.

**Remember, your journey *IS*
your destination.**